The ADVENT ADVENTURES

with FATHER NATE

By **Mia Toschi, Madalyn Jozaitis, & Saraidee Reyes-Villa**

Illustrated by **Amanda Jozaitis**

The Advent Adventures with Father Nate

Published by Gatekeeper Press
7853 Gunn Hwy., Suite 209
Tampa, FL 33626
www.GatekeeperPress.com

Library of Congress Control Number: 2024946729

ISBN (hardcover): 9781662954818
ISBN (paperback): 9781662952098
eISBN: 9781662954825

The ADVENT ADVENTURES with FATHER NATE

By Mia Toschi, Madalyn Jozaitis, & Saraidee Reyes-Villa

Illustrated by Amanda Jozaitis

Father Nate is a Catholic priest in a beautiful town with lots of lakes. His eyes are the color of the sky, his hair the color of the sun, and orange is the color of his favorite snack, carrots.
His friends call him a fit shepherd because he loves to exercise.

When he exercises, one of Father Nate's favorite things to do is find God's gifts that are everywhere.

When he rides his bike, he admires all of the flowers.

When he goes swimming on a hot day, he is thankful for the cool water.

When he hikes up a mountain, he makes friends with all the animals.

Father Nate begins each morning by saying the *Our Father* and giving thanks for all the wonderful things in his life.

What are you thankful for?

Can you **fold your hands in prayer** and say the *Our Father* with Father Nate?

Our Father,

Who art in heaven,
hallowed be Thy name.
Thy kingdom come; Thy will be
done on earth as it is in heaven.
Give us this day our daily bread,
and forgive us our trespasses as we
forgive those who trespass against us,
and lead us not into temptation,
but deliver us from evil.

Amen.

Father Nate is so happy because Christmas is coming. He and his friends decorate the church with lights and Christmas trees.

You will also see a green wreath with four candles. The wreath is round and has no beginning or end, just like Jesus' everlasting love has no beginning or end.

Each week Father Nate lights a new candle.

HOPE

Peace

Joy

Love

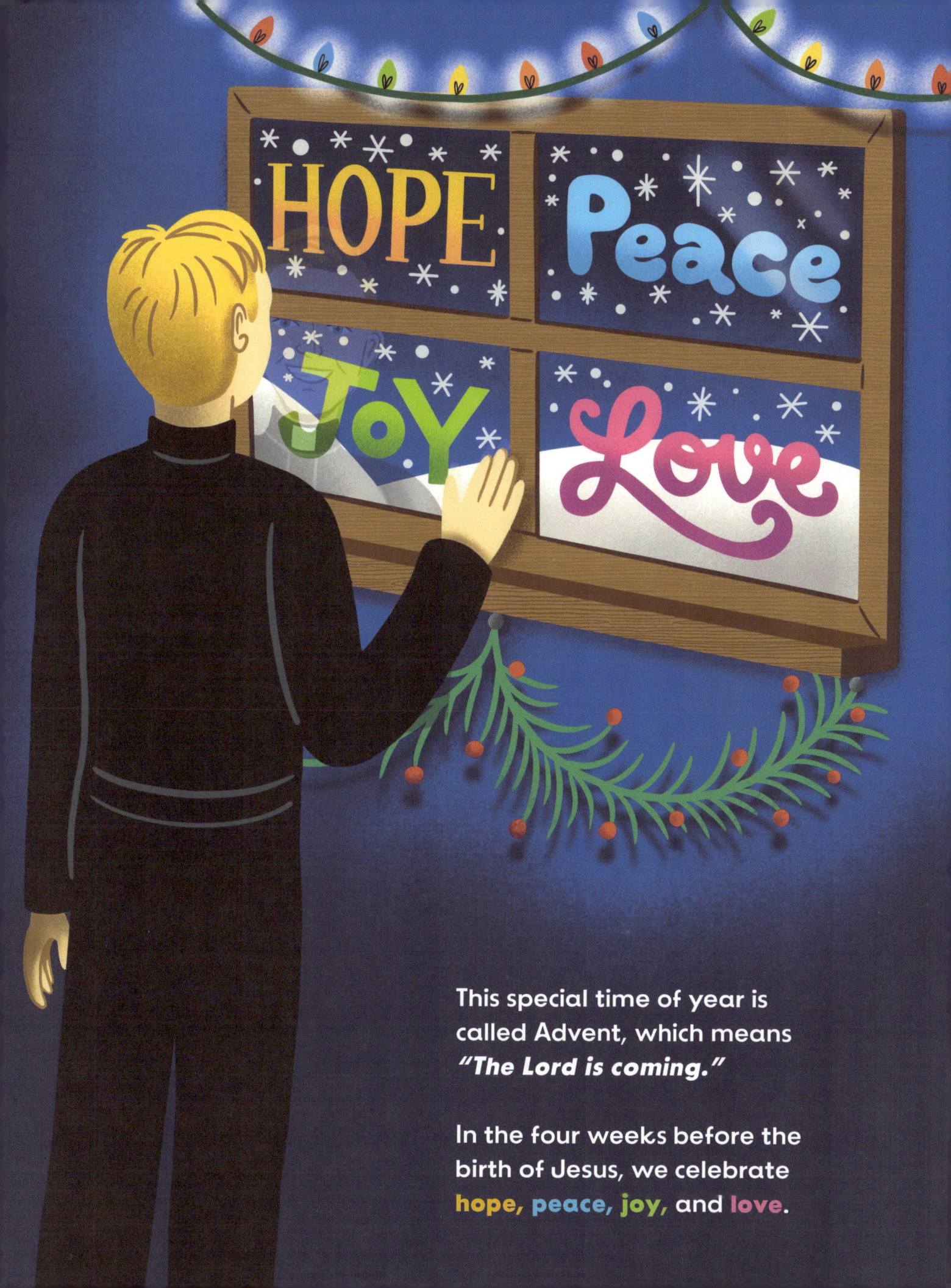

This special time of year is called Advent, which means *"The Lord is coming."*

In the four weeks before the birth of Jesus, we celebrate hope, peace, joy, and love.

During Advent, there is a special calendar that people use to count down the days leading up to Christmas. Father Nate opens up the tabs on his Advent calendar each day to reveal a special picture or message. It is a time to celebrate because baby Jesus will soon be born.

Here are some ways you can celebrate: **be kind, be thankful, and surround yourself with others who love Jesus.**

BE KIND

BE THANKFUL

LOVE JESUS

1 2 3 5
6 7 8 9 10
11 12 13 14 15
16 17 18 19 20
21 22 23 24 25

The church is very colorful during the Christmas season. Father Nate has many robes, which are called chasubles. During Advent priests wear purple and rose.

What other color chasuble does Father Nate have?

Purple is an important color during Advent. It signifies a time of prayer. The purple chasuble is worn to remind everyone of what we have done right and wrong and how we can help others.

Father Nate sends cards and bakes cookies which he shares.
How can you help your friends and family?

Father Nate also wears a rose chasuble during Advent. On the third Sunday during Advent, the color rose represents joy because baby Jesus is on the way!

During Advent there are special feast days Father Nate likes to celebrate. Let's look at the Advent calendar and see how each of these celebrations bring hope, peace, joy, and love to the world.

On December 6th, Father Nate celebrates Saint Nicholas. He was a kind man who helped others by giving gifts to the poor. Father Nate says, the truest gift lies in giving, not receiving. It is so much fun to give gifts, not just on Christmas, but every day!

On your Advent calendar you should mark **December 8th** for the Immaculate Conception. This day is a Holy Day of Obligation, which means everyone goes to Mass. On this day, we honor Mary, the Mother of God. For this reason, we say *"Hail Mary, full of grace."*

Hail Mary

Hail Mary, full of grace. The Lord is with thee. Blessed art thou amongst women, and blessed is the fruit of thy womb, Jesus. Holy Mary, Mother of God, pray for us sinners, now and at the hour of our death, Amen.

Another special day is **December 12**th. On this day, Mary appeared to a poor man, named Juan Diego, in Mexico.

Roses bloomed in the cold where Mary was seen. This was one of several miracles that took place. Mary's "image" appeared on Juan Diego's cloak.

This day is known as the **Feast day of Our Lady of Guadalupe.** During Mass, roses are distributed to the people to symbolize the miracles that were performed in Mexico.

This feast day is filled with peace and love. People gather with loved ones to share good food, listen to music, and play games. Piñatas are filled with special treats.

On December 13th, Saint Lucia is celebrated. In some countries girls wear wreaths with candles on their heads. The light reminds us that Jesus is the light of the world and brings hope.

What is your favorite Christmas tradition?

At the end of Advent on December 25th, baby Jesus is born in a manger in Bethlehem. It is a beautiful day because Jesus is Emmanuel, which means *"God is with us."* People join together at Mass to sing Christmas carols and celebrate the birth of Jesus. At church, you will see baby Jesus lying in the manger.

Can you write a greeting to baby Jesus?

After Mass, Father Nate visits his family. They play games, exchange presents, and have a big meal. Before they eat they pray together, saying, *"Bless us, O Lord, and these Thy gifts, which we are about to receive from Thy bounty, through Christ our Lord. Amen."*

Though Advent has ended, the Christmas season continues into the new year. On January 6th, we remember Three Kings Day, also known as the Feast of the Epiphany.

Many years ago, three kings were guided by a shining star that led them to baby Jesus in Bethlehem. Their names were **Caspar**, **Melchior**, and **Balthazar**, and they brought gifts for Jesus.

Father Nate celebrates this day by blessing chalk. Members of the church use this chalk to bless their homes for the new year.

In Latin, the initials **C+M+B** stand for Christus Mansionem Benedicat. This means, *"May Christ bless this home."*

Father Nate says, *"May God bless your home, your family, and bring you* hope, peace, joy, *and* love *this Christmas season and every day throughout the year."*

About the Authors & Illustrator

Mia Toschi is a four-time Emmy-winning television news reporter who has shared stories about faith from all over the world. Mia has a master's in Education and is a parishioner and volunteer at her local parish in Indiana. This is her third book and second children's book.

Madalyn Jozaitis is the Director of Religious Education and Office Manager for her home parish in Indiana. She is also a former teacher in both elementary and special education. Her passion is in guiding children through their faith journey and helping form them as disciples.

Saraidee Reyes-Villa is a college student currently pursuing her degree in Communications. She is also the Faith Formation and Communications Assistant at her home parish in Indiana. Her passion lies in working with children and hopes to become a missionary when she graduates.

Amanda Jozaitis is a designer and illustrator in Indiana. Known for her vibrant, playful, contemporary style, she incorporates intricate details, textures, and hand lettering inspired by vintage design.

This book was put together to teach children about the Catholic faith and to help form them as disciples. It teaches children about the joy of giving and introduces them to saints celebrated throughout Advent.

Father Nate is a Catholic parish priest in Indiana.

A portion of the proceeds of this book are dedicated to Catholic education for children.

www.ingramcontent.com/pod-product-compliance
Lightning Source LLC
LaVergne TN
LVHW071826151224
799168LV00003B/144